Staying Safe in Emergencies

by Robin Nelson

Series consultants: Sonja Green, MD, and
Distinguished Professor Emerita Ann Nolte, PhD

Lerner Books • London • New York • Minneapolis

Text copyright © 2006 by Lerner Publishing Group, Inc.

This book was first published in the United States of America in 2006.

First published in the United Kingdom in 2008 by
Lerner Books,
Dalton House,
60 Windsor Avenue,
London SW19 2RR

Website address: www.lernerbooks.co.uk

This edition was updated and edited for UK publication by Discovery Books Ltd., Unit 3, 37 Watling Street, Leintwardine, Shropshire SY7 0LW

Words in **bold** type are explained in a glossary on page 31.

British Library Cataloguing in Publication Data

Nelson, Robin, 1971-
   Staying safe in emergencies. - (Pull ahead Books. Health)
   1. Emergencies - Juvenile literature
   I. Title
   613.6

   ISBN-13: 978 1 58013 406 4

Printed in China

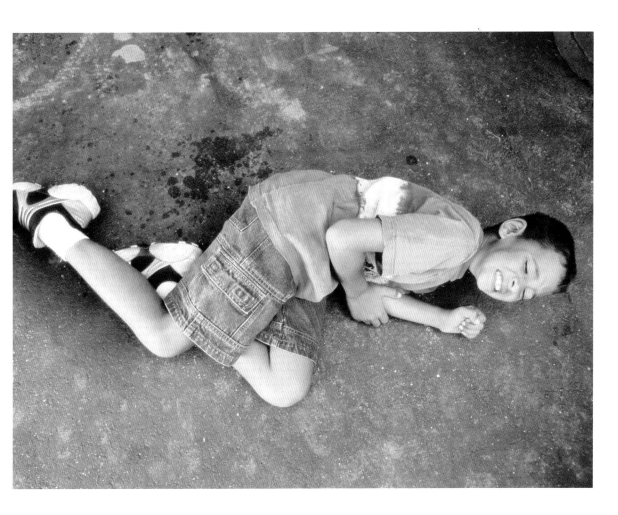

Help! **Emergency!**

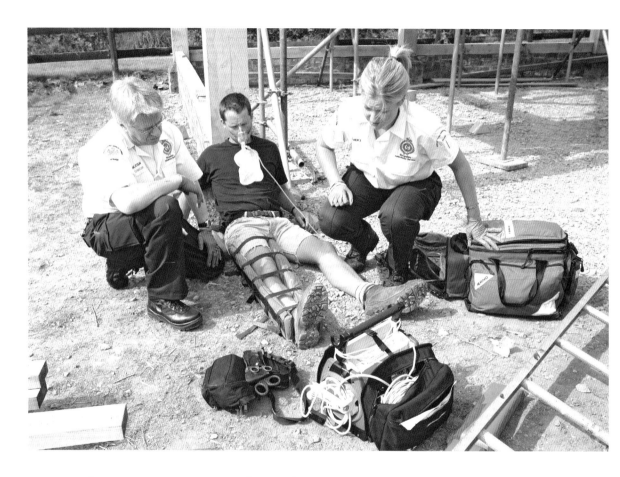

An emergency is when someone is
badly hurt or in danger.

It is an emergency when someone is bleeding a lot or has a broken bone. When someone can't breathe well or is **unconscious,** it is an emergency.

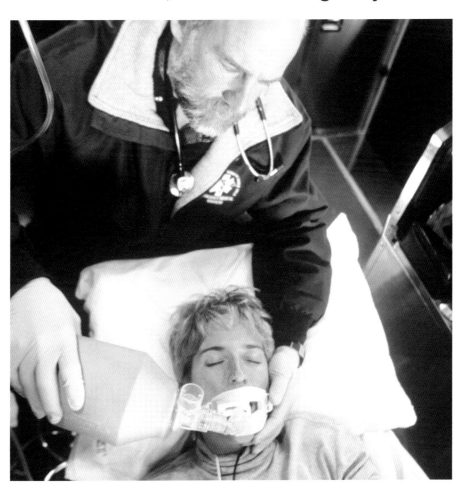

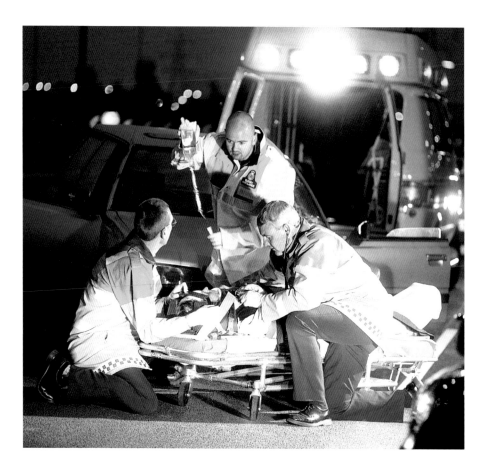

Sometimes **accidents** happen. It is
important to be ready.

Do you know what to do in an emergency?

Try to stay calm. Find an adult or shout for help.

8

If an adult is not near, you can
telephone for help. Do you know how?
Dial 999.

The person who answers a 999 call will ask you your name. He or she will ask what happened and where you are. You must speak clearly and slowly.

The person on the phone will send
the police, the fire service or an
ambulance. Stay on the phone until
help arrives.

Should you call 999 if you fall off your bike and scrape your knee? No, a scraped knee is not an emergency. Instead, find an adult to help you.

Only call 999 in an emergency. If you are not sure if it is an emergency? It is better to be safe and call 999.

Fire! What should you do? Go
outside straight away! Call 999 from a
neighbour's house.

If your clothes are on fire, remember
'stop, drop and roll!' Stop straight
away, drop to the floor and start to roll.
This puts out the fire.

There are
ways you
can help
when
someone
gets hurt.

Learning **first aid** can help you take care of simple **injuries.** What are some ways to give first aid?

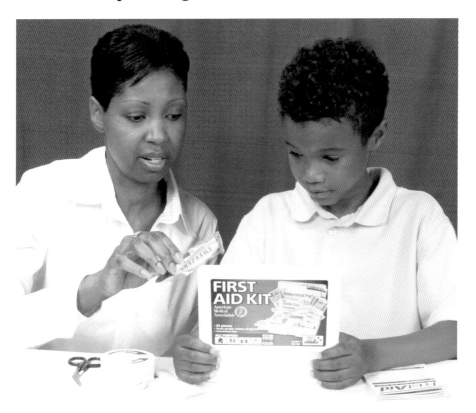

Ouch! Matt cut his finger. It is bleeding. What should you do?

Shout for help. Get a clean cloth.
Press the cloth on the cut. Keep
pressing until the bleeding stops or
until help comes.

Ouch! Maggie touched a hot pan on the cooker. She burnt her hand. It is turning red. What should you do?

Run some cold water in the sink. Tell Maggie to put her hand in the cold water. Her hand will feel better. Find an adult to help.

Megan fell down and hurt her arm! She can't move it. What should you do?

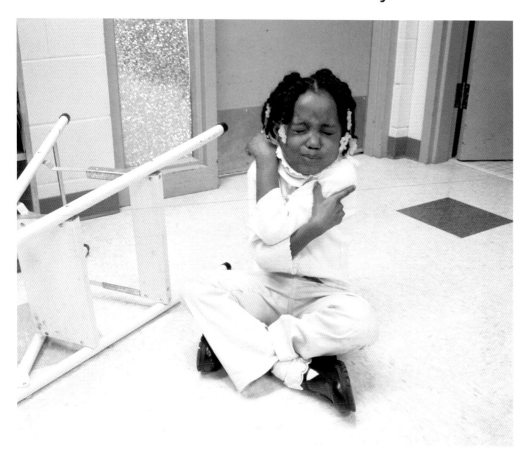

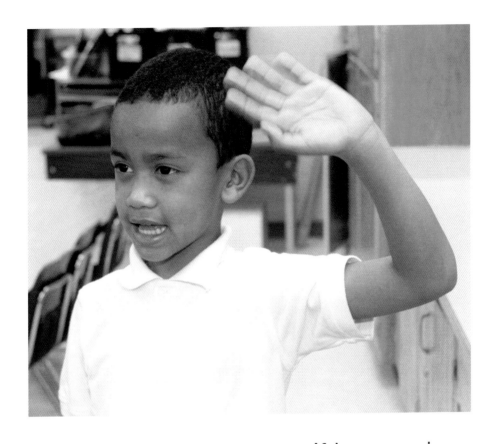

Tell Megan not to move. If her arm is broken, moving it will make it worse. Run and find an adult to help.

Oh, no! Tommy ate something from the medicine shelf. It could be **poisonous.** What should you do?

Take the
bottle away.
Call 999.

How else can you be ready? Practise what to do in emergencies. Make a first aid kit. Keep a list of important numbers near the phone.

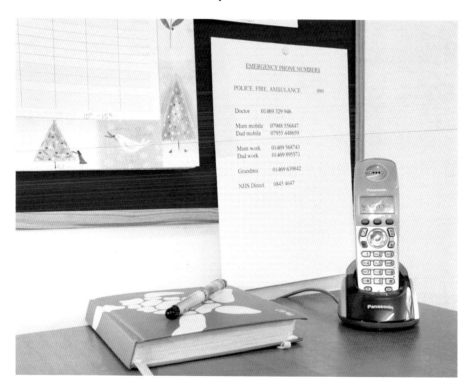

Being prepared for an emergency is the best way to stay safe!

First Aid Kit

You can be ready for an emergency by making a first aid kit. Use a box or other container. You will need an adult to help you. First put in a list of emergency phone numbers. Include 999 and the phone numbers for your doctor, the hospital and a family member. Here are some good things to put in your first aid kit:

- plasters in several sizes

- medical tape

- gauze rolls and pads

- cotton wool balls

- latex or vinyl gloves

- safety pins

- clean tissues

- tweezers

- small scissors

- nail clippers

- hot/cold instant packs

- antiseptic ointments and creams

- hand sanitizer

- antiseptic wipes

- allergy medication like Benadryl

- pain relievers

- petroleum jelly

Books and Websites

Books

Hunter, Rebecca. *Paramedic* (People Who Help Us) Cherrytree Books, 2006.

Mitton, Tony. *Flashing Fire Engines* (Amazing Machines) Kingfisher Books Ltd, 2007.

Oliver, Clare. *Ambulance Crew* (People Who Help Us) Franklin Watts, 2007.

Oxlade, Chris. *Emergency Vehicles* (Transport Around the World) Heinemann Library, 2002.

Websites

Crucial crew
http://crucial-crew.org

Welltown
http://www.welltown.gov.uk/home/kitchen.htm

Glossary

accidents: events that happen unexpectedly and often involve someone being hurt

ambulance: a car or van that picks up sick or injured people and takes them to the hospital

emergency: a problem that could be dangerous and that must be dealt with quickly

first aid: care given to an ill or injured person before he or she is looked at by a doctor

injuries: cuts, scrapes, bruises, breaks or physical harm

poisonous: harmful or dangerous if swallowed, breathed in or touched

unconscious: not awake, not able to see, feel, hear or think

Index

ambulance 11

broken bones 5, 22–23
burns 20–21

cuts 5, 18–19

dialing 999 9–11, 12, 13, 14, 25

emergencies 3, 4–5, 12

fire safety 14–15

first aid 17, 18–25
first aid kit 26, 28–29

999 operator 10–11

poisoning 24–25
preparing for emergencies 26, 28–29

responding to emergencies 7–9, 13, 22–23, 24–25, 26, 28

Photo Acknowledgements

The photographs in this book appear with the permission of: © Todd Strand/Independent Picture Service, cover, pp 9, 10, 15, 17, 19, 23, 25; © Neal & Molly Jansen/SuperStock, p 3; © Chris Fairclough/Discovery Picture Library, pp 4, 11; © Tom Stewart/CORBIS, p 5; © PhotoDisc/Getty Images, pp 6, 13; © age fotostock/SuperStock, p 7; © Royalty-Free/CORBIS, p 8; © Layne Kennedy/CORBIS, p 12; © Robert Llewellyn/SuperStock, p 14; © Mark Clarke/Photo Researchers, Inc., p 16; © Sam Lund/Independent Picture Service, pp 18, 22, 27; © Bsip, Laurent/Photo Researchers, Inc., p 20; © Heide Benser/zefa/Corbis, p 21; © David Woods/CORBIS, p 24; © Bobby Humphrey/Discovery Books, p 26.